AMERICA
AN AMAZING PLACE

Natalie Danford

America

An Amazing Place

CHARTWELL
BOOKS

P. 2: THE STATUE OF LIBERTY HAS
WELCOMED IMMIGRANTS TO AMERICAN
SHORES SINCE 1886.
OPPOSITE: AT HORSESHOE BEND IN
ARIZONA, THE COLORADO RIVER TURNS
SHARPLY.
PP. 6-7: THE FOUR PRESIDENTS CARVED
INTO MOUNT RUSHMORE ARE LIT BY
SETTING SUN.
PP. 8-9: THE ICONIC MANHATTAN SKYLINE,
SEEN ACROSS THE HUDSON RIVER,
REPRESENTS MODERNITY AROUND THE
WORLD.

OPPOSITE: THE MANHATTAN SKYLINE AND OTHER
LANDMARKS ARE REINTERPRETED IN OVER-THE-TOP LAS
VEGAS.
PP. 12-13: A ROCK FORMATION FRAMES A VIEW IN
CANYONLANDS NATIONAL PARK.

OPPOSITE: SAN FRANCISCO'S FAMOUS
ORANGE GOLDEN GATE BRIDGE SEEMS TO
GLOW AT DUSK.
PP. 16-17: THE DOWNTOWN CHICAGO
WATERFRONT TEEMS WITH ACTIVITY.

CONTENTS

PACIFIC
WEST

CANADA

New England

Pacific West

Midwest

Mid-Atlantic

Mountain West

South

Pacific West

MEXICO

CUBA

INTRODUCTION

Generalizing about the United States of America is nearly impossible. As its name implies, the country is composed of 50 disparate states. Each has its own government (a sort of miniature version of the country's government, with the governor standing in as "president" of the state), its own flag and motto and animal and tree and flower and official nickname. Each state even has its own song. More importantly, each has its own personality—its quirky features and foods and traditions. Sometimes, considering all of these individual characteristics, it's amazing the country exists at all. Yet exist it does—with a brashness and self-confidence that sometimes reads as arrogance to those of other nationalities.

In this book, the 50 states have been arranged into the commonly used, though unofficial, regions loosely grouped by geography and climate. Of course, borders are always imposed by humans, but many of the borders between the American states are natural—rivers and mountain ranges, lakes and valleys created natural dividing lines between some of the states. Some states have unusual shapes that can be traced to historic origins, like the Oklahoma "panhandle," a rectangle of land that was neutral territory until Oklahoma was granted statehood in 1907 and took it over.

The American Revolution, which lasted from 1775 to 1783, began as a war against Britain by 13 British colonies in what we now know as the United States. The country we know today blossomed gradually as various states were added at different times and under different circumstances. Some territories were won in war; others, like the state of Louisiana, were purchased. This, too, accounts for the diversity of cultures.

The United States has always been a country of immigrants, beginning with those first settlers and explorers. In the late 19th and early 20th centuries, the country experienced a flood of immigrants, many of them Italian, Irish or Jewish. Most Americans are descended from people born elsewhere. And active immigration continues. In modern-day New York City, one out of every three residents is an immigrant; the New York City borough of Queens is considered the most ethnically diverse place in the world, and 48 percent of its 2.2 million residents were born outside of the United States. They speak 138 different languages. That's an extreme example of the kind of diversity found in the country as a whole, but the more than 300 million Americans who populate the country's 3,794,083 square miles (9,826,630 square kilometers), represent a wide range of backgrounds, justly earning the country a reputation as a "melting pot."

That's just one of the many nicknames and catchphrases attached to the nation. The United States is also referred to as a "grand experiment," because it was believed to be the first country to attempt to function as a democracy. The success or failure of that attempt can be debated, but that effort to create a nation that was ever looking forward, a place where a person's origins did not dictate his destiny, and a place, as Martin Luther King, Jr. put it in his famous 1963 "I Have a Dream" speech delivered to an audience of 250,000 on the Washington, D.C. mall, where people would "not be judged by the color of their skin, but by the content of their character," has also had tremendous impact on the nation's evolution. No doubt, there have been shameful episodes in the history of the United States—the near obliteration of the indigenous people by European settlers, slavery, the internment of Japanese-Americans during World War II. But Americans never fail to look toward the future and to keep striving, whether toward their own financial success or artistic achievement or to create better lives for subsequent generations.

Because the United States so dominated world culture and especially entertainment in the 20th century, much of it can seem familiar. Visitors to New York, Los Angeles, Chicago and other areas often find that they feel they are in a movie, as the landmarks, the sounds and even the people themselves are so recognizable from film and television. But there is much to be discovered in both places that are heavily featured and those that are more obscure. The details, the scale (often enormous) and the beauty of even familiar locales hold surprises. The individuality and specificity of the states and the regions they form make for natural and manmade landscapes as varied as Americans themselves. In the end, though it sounds like a contradiction in terms, the one thing the 50 states share just may be their diversity—and diversity is perhaps the most American quality of all.

P. 20-21: NEW YORK CITY'S TIMES SQUARE IS FILLED WITH HUSTLE AND BUSTLE DAY AND NIGHT.
P. 22-23: BRYCE CANYON NATIONAL PARK IN UTAH BOASTS MILES AND MILES OF DRAMATIC ROCK FORMATIONS.

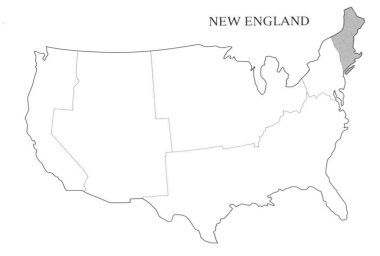

NEW ENGLAND

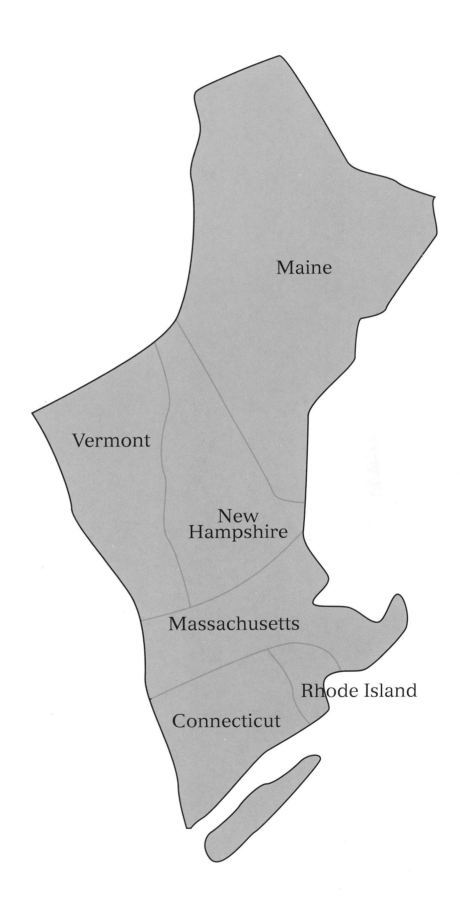

Maine

Vermont

New
Hampshire

Massachusetts

Rhode Island

Connecticut

NEW ENGLAND

WHERE IT ALL BEGAN

The six states that make up the mountainous terrain of the New England region were among the first British colonies in the New World, and New England was the first clearly defined region in the United States. Not only is the very name of the area intended to represent a new start for people from England, but one of the states—New Hampshire—and many of its towns—including New London, Connecticut—were named after British cities.

It was in New England that most of the major battles of the American Revolutionary War were fought. Inhabitants of the area still have a fiercely independent spirit that stretches back to before the colonial era. The Pilgrims, a group of religious separatists who came from England via Holland in the 1600s, are generally considered to have been the first European settlers in what is now the United States. (Obviously, as was the case everywhere, the land was already inhabited by indigenous peoples, including the Pequot and Wampanoag tribes.) The Pilgrims arrived on the Mayflower in Plymouth in what is now Massachusetts and celebrated a day of gratitude that has been transformed over the years into one of the few truly American holidays—Thanksgiving.

The Massachusetts Bay Colony was founded in the late 1620s, and its capital city, Boston, was founded in 1630. The colony was basically a theocracy run by Puritans (an even larger group of strict religionists than the Pilgrims), who, though they had come seeking religious freedom, were rather intolerant of other religions. The colony was also an economic undertaking, and quite a successful one. It was here, too, that the rebellion against the British and the cry that there should be "no taxation without representation" took root and festered, with events such as the Boston Tea Party—when locals dumped tea into the harbor rather than pay the taxes demanded from them—and the Battle of Bunker Hill in Charlestown. The Old North Church, an Episcopal church in Boston, is said to have been the site from which the signal of "one if by land and two if by sea"—in reference to the arrival of the British army—was indicated with lanterns in the bell tower.

Boston remains a colonial city in appearance today, though it has its share of modern buildings, including the 60-story Hancock Place completed in 1977, the tallest building in the entire New England region. No one visits Boston to look at a glass skyscraper, however. It's the small, tidy city's older buildings and neighborhoods that attract visitors, from the shops on tony Newbury Street, to charming Beacon Hill, to Boston's own Little Italy in the North End. The Boston Common, which dates back to 1634, making it the oldest park in the United States, is centrally located and the most famous park in the series of parks and other green spaces known as the Emerald Necklace. Many sites in Boston are the oldest of their kind, including Fenway Park, the oldest Major League baseball stadium still in use. The Red Sox played their first game there in 1912.

OPPOSITE: THE *MAYFLOWER II*,
DOCKED IN PLYMOUTH,
MASSACHUSETTS, IS A FULL-SCALE
REPLICA OF THE *MAYFLOWER*, THE
SHIP THAT CARRIED SOME OF THE FIRST
EUROPEAN SETTLERS TO WHAT IS
TODAY THE UNITED STATES.
ABOVE: THIS IS THE TYPE OF HUT THAT
THE EARLY SETTLERS USED.

Both of Boston and apart from it is the city of Cambridge, forever linked with the most famous university in the United States and one of the most famous in the world, Harvard University. Established in 1636, Harvard is also the oldest university in the United States. Its illustrious alumni form a long list of names in politics, the arts and other fields. Also located in Cambridge is the prestigious Massachusetts Institute of Technology, a university founded in 1861 with an emphasis on science and engineering. These are just two better known examples of the many universities—large and small, public and private—that dot the New

ABOVE AND OPPOSITE: THE BACK BAY AND BEACON HILL
NEIGHBORHOODS OF BOSTON HAVE RETAINED THE CITY'S HISTORICAL
CHARM, EVEN AS SKYSCRAPERS HAVE SPRUNG UP AROUND THEM.

OPPOSITE: THE OLD STATE HOUSE IN
BOSTON, MASSACHUSETTS WAS BUILT IN
1713 AND IS THE OLDEST SURVIVING
PUBLIC BUILDING IN BOSTON. TODAY IT
HOUSES A MUSEUM.
P. 32: COPLEY SQUARE IN CENTRAL
BOSTON IS BORDERED BY OLD AND NEW
BUILDINGS, INCLUDING TRINITY CHURCH,
ON THE LEFT, AND HANCOCK PLACE, ON
THE RIGHT.
P. 33: THE "NEW" MASSACHUSETTS STATE
HOUSE SITS ATOP BOSTON'S BEACON HILL
AND BOASTS A COPPER DOME COVERED IN
GOLD.
PP. 34-35: BOSTON MIXES OLD AND NEW
ARCHITECTURE WITH APLOMB.

OPPOSITE: THE BOSTON PUBLIC GARDEN
PROVIDES GREEN RESPITE IN THE HEART OF
THE CITY.

England region. Harvard's arch-rival, Yale University, was founded in New Haven, Connecticut in 1701 and boasts a spectacular campus in the style known as Collegiate Gothic. The university also has several notable modern buildings, including Paul Rudolph's Art and Architecture Building and two modern residential buildings designed by Eero Saarinen. The Yale Art Gallery was recently renovated, and the original Louis Kahn building combined with other existing buildings to exhibit the university's impressive collection of modern and older works.

Elsewhere in Connecticut, in New Canaan, Philip Johnson's Glass House is open for visits. Now a National

Trust Historic Site, the house was completed in 1949 and has no interior walls and only glass walls on the exterior, a radical idea at the time (and still today for anyone who values privacy). The architect used the house as his own residence, and it is a landmark in contemporary architecture. The 47-acre property includes several other buildings.

Boston, which sits right on the water, dominates the eastern part of Massachusetts. The state's curling "arm" projects out into the Atlantic, and the tip of that piece of land is the area known as Cape Cod, with many charming beach towns along the ocean. Off the coast of Cape Cod are the two islands of Martha's Vineyard and

ABOVE: BOSTON'S FENWAY PARK HAS BEEN HOME TO THE CITY'S BELOVED RED SOX BASEBALL TEAM SINCE 1912.

Nantucket, once homes to the captains of whaling ships (in the classic American novel *Moby Dick,* the whaling ship the Pequod departs from Nantucket) and today some of the most lovely American vacation spots, crisscrossed by bike paths and favored by the East coast elite.

The western part of Massachusetts has more in common with the rest of New England, as it is a more rural and mountainous area with plenty of natural attractions. The Berkshires, a hilly region that crosses from western Massachusetts into Connecticut, lie in the picturesque western part of the state. Opportunities for hiking and fishing abound in the Berkshires, and Mass

MoCA, as the Massachusetts Museum of Contemporary Art in North Adams, Massachusetts is known, opened in 1999 and hosts both art exhibits and live performances. More performances—generally of a more classical nature—have been taking place at Tanglewood in western Massachusetts since the 1850s, and many of the performances here are outdoors.

Though it's true that New England has more than its fair share of universities, much of the region's allure stems from its natural sites. New Hampshire has the White Mountains; Vermont has the Green Mountains and Lake Champlain. Both states are favorite sites to visit in the fall, when the foliage is spectacular, and miles of

maple trees appear to glow orange and red. Those trees are also "tapped" for the naturally occurring sweet sap that is then boiled into maple syrup and served over traditional American breakfast dishes, such as pancakes. Both of these northern states are also known for their many covered bridges. Like Massachusetts, the rest of the region was active in the American Revolution. Many modern residents of New Hampshire still fly the state's flag with its rebellious slogan, *Live Free or Die*. New Hampshire is also the location of the country's first presidential primary every four years, so it has taken on a greater significance in national politics than its small size and population—a little over 1,300,000 according

to the 2012 census—merits.

Maine, the figurehead at the country's prow, is similar to New Hampshire and Vermont, but it enjoys a long coastline that tends to be rocky rather than sandy. The Maine coastline is a source for many of New England's lobsters. Maine is also home to the almost 50,000-acre (192 square kilometers) Acadia National Park, the oldest national park east of the Mississippi River.

Tiny Rhode Island is also part of New England. Rhode Island is the smallest state in the nation in size. Despite its name, Rhode Island is not an island, but sits tucked under Massachusetts along the coast of the

OPPOSITE: CAMBRIDGE, MASSACHUSETTS
IS HOME TO TWO TOP-TIER UNIVERSITIES:
THE MASSACHUSETTS INSTITUTE OF
TECHNOLOGY AND HARVARD.

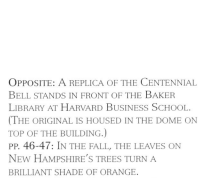

OPPOSITE: A REPLICA OF THE CENTENNIAL
BELL STANDS IN FRONT OF THE BAKER
LIBRARY AT HARVARD BUSINESS SCHOOL.
(THE ORIGINAL IS HOUSED IN THE DOME ON
TOP OF THE BUILDING.)

PP. 46-47: IN THE FALL, THE LEAVES ON
NEW HAMPSHIRE'S TREES TURN A
BRILLIANT SHADE OF ORANGE.

PP. 48-49: THE ANDROSCOGGIN RIVER IN
NORTHERN NEW HAMPSHIRE REFLECTS
FALL FOLIAGE.

PP. 50-51: PORTLAND, MAINE IS HOME TO
THE PORTLAND HEAD LIGHT, ONE OF THE
MANY LIGHTHOUSES ALONG THE STATE'S
ROCKY COAST.

P. 52: LOBSTER FLOATS HANG ON THE SIDE
OF A HOUSE ON MOUNT DESERT ISLAND IN
MAINE.

P. 53: MAINE IS JUSTLY FAMOUS FOR ITS
LOBSTER INDUSTRY.

P. 54: JORDAN POND IN ACADIA NATIONAL
PARK OFFERS SERENE VISTAS.

P. 55: THE BASS HARBOR HEAD LIGHT, A
CLASSIC NEW ENGLAND LIGHTHOUSE,
GLOWS AT DAWN.

Opposite: Pemaquid Point Lighthouse,
Bristol Maine.

OPPOSITE: THE SANKATY HEAD LIGHT
ON THE ISLAND OF NANTUCKET, WAS
BUILT IN 1850.
ABOVE: MARTHA'S VINEYARD, AN
ISLAND OFF THE COAST OF NEW
ENGLAND, IS DOTTED WITH VICTORIAN
GINGERBREAD HOUSES.

OPPOSITE: IN THE FALL, NEW
ENGLAND TOWNS LIKE CHESTER,
MASSACHUSETTS ARE GRACED WITH
BRILLIANTLY COLORED FOLIAGE.
ABOVE: EVEN AN ABANDONED
COTTAGE IN THE WOODS LOOKS
INVITING DURING PEAK FOLIAGE
SEASON IN NEW ENGLAND.

PP. 62-63: MOUNT MANSFIELD
SERVES AS A BACKDROP TO LEAVES
CHANGING THEIR COLORS IN STOWE,
VERMONT.

mainland United States. Rhode Island was actually the first state to declare independence from the British, and it has the character of a terrier—small but tough and determined to assert itself. Rhode Island is also known as a place of religious tolerance. The first Jewish synagogue in the United States, Touro Synagogue, was founded in Newport, Rhode Island, in 1759, and the state often served as a refuge from the stern rule of the Puritans in the pre-colonial era. In the mid-19th century, the town of Newport, Rhode Island began to develop as a popular resort town, and as the years went on, wealthy industrialists and their families built mansions in Newport that rivaled Versailles (and indeed in the case of at least one were modeled after it). One branch of the Vanderbilt family built the 70-room mansion known as The Breakers; a silver heiress commissioned Rosecliff and then threw parties with entertainment by the likes of Harry Houdini. Today many of these "cottages," as the owners termed them, despite their mammoth size, have been transformed into house-museums.

ABOVE: THE WHITE MOUNTAINS OF NEW HAMPSHIRE ARE STUNNING IN AUTUMN.
PP. 66-67: PROVIDENCE, RHODE ISLAND WAS ONE OF THE FIRST CITIES ESTABLISHED IN THE UNITED STATES.

MID-ATLANTIC

New York

New Jersey

Pennsylvania

Delaware

Maryland

Washington, DC

Mid-Atlantic

Big Cities and Small Towns

The Mid-Atlantic states, along the eastern seaboard in the United States, include one locale that can only be considered what Americans call "an 800-pound gorilla" (The expression derives from a very old riddle: *Where does an 800-pound gorilla sit? Anywhere it wants to.*) That 800-pound gorilla would be, of course, New York City, the largest city in the United States, one of the largest in the world, and an unstoppable force that tends to overshadow anything in its vicinity.

As Frank Sinatra so famously sang, "If you can make it here, you'll make it anywhere." And as Grandmaster Flash rapped at a later date, "New York, New York, big city of dreams. And everything in New York ain't always what it seems." New York is a symbol of the modern metropolis and of modernity and industry itself. Its iconic skyline is full of classic buildings and structures known around the world. The Empire State Building, the Chrysler Building, the New York Stock Exchange, the New York Public Library, the Mies van der Rohe and Philip Johnson designed Seagram Building—a list of important works of architecture in New York could fill a book and has filled many. But it's not just the older buildings that appeal—the most famous contemporary architects (jokingly dubbed "starchitects") vie to design buildings in New York as well: Frank Gehry's 8 Spruce Street twists into the sky in lower Manhattan, and Renzo Piano designed the *New York Times* building erected in the early 2000s. The Freedom Tower, a 104-story skyscraper built to replace the Twin Towers after

they were destroyed in a 2001 terrorist attack, is one of the more high-profile modern additions.

Visitors may see the city as a monolithic place, but New Yorkers themselves are constantly dividing up the city to make it more manageable. New York City consists of five boroughs: Manhattan, Brooklyn, Queens, the Bronx and Staten Island. Then each of those can be broken down further into neighborhoods: Little Italy, Chinatown, charming Greenwich Village and so on. Since the days when it was known as New Amsterdam, New York has been fast-changing and ever-evolving. The first settlements in Manhattan were farms at the southern tip of the island. Development moved northward (or *uptown,* as New Yorkers would describe it) with each passing year. Central Park, once a shantytown, was transformed into a 778-acre urban park. In 1858, Frederick Law Olmsted and Calvert Vaux won a design competition and proceeded to remake it into a stunning pastoral green space laced with walking paths and graceful bridges. SoHo (an abbreviation for South of Houston), a derelict neighborhood of abandoned factories, was taken over by artists in the 1960s and 1970s and today the lofts in its cast-iron buildings are some of the most expensive real estate in the world. More recent sites of this kind of rapid gentrification and development include Williamsburg, a neighborhood on the western edge of Brooklyn that has become a hothouse for youthful experimentation, and DUMBO (short for Down

PP. 70-71: At sunset, light reflects off of buildings in midtown Manhattan.
PP. 72-73: New York City's Times Square is famous for its fast pace, gigantic billboards and Broadway theaters.

ABOVE: AN AMERICAN FLAG HANGS ON THE FRONT OF THE NEW YORK STOCK
EXCHANGE IN NEW YORK CITY'S FINANCIAL DISTRICT.
OPPOSITE: THE CHRYSLER BUILDING, A PRIME EXAMPLE OF ART DECO
ARCHITECTURE, WAS DESIGNED BY WILLIAM VAN ALEN. ALTHOUGH IT HAS NOT
BEEN THE TALLEST BUILDING IN NEW YORK CITY SINCE 1931, ITS GRACEFUL LINES
MAKE IT A LOCAL FAVORITE.

ABOVE: AT NIGHT, NEW YORK CITY'S
SKYSCRAPERS TWINKLE IN THE DARK.
OPPOSITE: THE *NEW YORK TIMES*
BUILDING, COMPLETED IN 2007, IS
SEEN HERE FROM THE EMPIRE STATE
BUILDING.

THE SOLOMON R GUGGENHEIM MUSEUM

Under the Manhattan Bridge Overpass), where subway trains rumble overhead and an extensive park and modern carousel sit alongside the water.

Manhattan is the central borough of New York City. It is also the smallest and the most densely populated. Because it is an island, it has a series of bridges and tunnels around its perimeter. The most iconic is the Brooklyn Bridge, the suspension bridge completed in 1883 that connects Manhattan to Brooklyn.

New York's museums are world-class and numerous, from the Metropolitan Museum of Art, one of the world's three largest museums, which was built in 1874, to the Museum of Modern Art, opened in the early 1900s and expanded by Yoshio Taniguchi in 1997, to the Guggenheim Museum, housed in a unique cylindrical building designed by Frank Lloyd Wright. Collections reach beyond the fine arts: The Museum of Natural History boasts a collection of more than 32 million specimens, and the New York Transit Museum

provides an overview of the city's tremendous subway system—the world's largest (and one of its oldest) with more than 400 stations. The first line of the subway opened in 1904 (initially, the lines were separate and privately owned), and new lines are still being added today.

New York City sits in the state of New York. (This dual meaning of "New York," as both the name of the city and the name of the state can sometimes cause confusion, and it inspired one of the city's nicknames: The City So Nice They Named It Twice.) Much of the state of New York provides rural contrast to the teeming metropolis. The state runs all the way up to the Canadian border, where it shares Niagara Falls with the province of Ontario. The verdant Catskill Mountains take up much of the southeastern portion of the state, and Long Island and the tony beach towns in the Hamptons stretch east of the city into the Atlantic Ocean. The Hudson River cuts almost vertically along

ABOVE: THE GUGGENHEIM MUSEUM IN NEW YORK CITY IS FAMOUS FOR ITS CYLINDRICAL SHAPE; IT WAS DESIGNED BY FRANK LLOYD WRIGHT.
OPPOSITE: THE FREEDOM TOWER STANDS 104 STORIES TALL.
P. 80: IN NEW YORK'S SOHO (WHICH STANDS FOR SOUTH OF HOUSTON STREET) NEIGHBORHOOD, FIRE ESCAPES ZIGZAG UP AND DOWN BUILDING FACADES.
P. 81: THE FLATIRON BUILDING IN MANHATTAN—NAMED FOR ITS UNUSUAL TRIANGULAR SHAPE—WAS DESIGNATED A NEW YORK CITY LANDMARK IN 1966.
PP. 82-83: THE WORLD TRADE CENTER SITE IS LIT BY TWO BLUE BEAMS TO REPRESENT THE LOST TWIN TOWERS. IN THE FOREGROUND STANDS THE BROOKLYN BRIDGE.

the eastern portion of the state, and the Erie Canal, dug from 1817 to 1825, runs horizontally and was a great boon to 19th-century industry, as it connected Albany to Buffalo, making it possible for goods to reach the Great Lakes region of the United States from the Atlantic Ocean, traveling solely by water.

South of New York is the state of Pennsylvania, home to the city of Philadelphia. In many other parts of the country, Philadelphia would be considered a metropolis, but it is somewhat overshadowed by the gorilla to its north. Philadelphia's glory days were in the colonial and post-colonial era. The Declaration of Independence was signed there in Independence Hall (visitors still flock to see the Liberty Bell, which was rung to celebrate the establishment of the nation). From 1790 to 1800, Philadelphia was the capital of the United States. Known as the City of Brotherly Love (a literal translation of the city's Greek moniker), Philadelphia has its own Robert Indiana *LOVE* sculpture and a museum district with a fine museum of art and

the Franklin Institute, an excellent science museum, named for Benjamin Franklin, a member of the group known as the Founding Fathers and a strong proponent of American independence as well as an inventor and writer.

Another innovative thinker, artist Andy Warhol, was a native of the still smaller city of Pittsburgh, Pennsylvania, once an industrial powerhouse and home to the Andy Warhol Museum. And yet another home in Pennsylvania that merits mention is Fallingwater, the multi-layered Frank Lloyd Wright house that appears to balance delicately over a waterfall.

Further south still is Washington, D.C., the nation's capital. This unique "federal city" was created separate from any state, with the idea that it could house the nation's government and remain unbiased. Residents of D.C. (which stands for the District of Columbia) might argue whether or not that experiment has been a success, but there is no denying the impact of the many monuments and impressive buildings in

Washington, D.C., starting with the White House, the home to the American president.

The White House was designed by James Hoban and completed in 1800, and it is a symbol recognized around the world. The enormous complex includes both living quarters for the presidential family and plenty of office space. The Rose Garden is a favorite spot for press conferences, and the president's desk is located in the Oval Office, which was designed in this unusual shape for the purposes of the formal receptions once held there.

Washington, D.C. is a city of monuments, too. The National Mall is a rectangular lawn dotted with monuments, including the Washington Monument, a gigantic obelisk honoring the country's first president, the Lincoln Memorial, dedicated to the 16th president

of the United States in 1922 and Maya Lin's Vietnam Veterans Memorial, a somber black slab with the names of more than 50,000 soldiers killed in the war. Lin was only 21 and still a college student in 1981, when her design was selected from close to 1,500 submissions. Public opinion was divided on the unusual memorial (just as public opinion in the United States about the Vietnam War was and remains sharply divided), and as a result a very traditional bronze statue titled *The Three Soldiers* was erected nearby as a concession to those who objected.

Also on the National Mall are several popular (and free-of-charge) museums that are part of the Smithsonian Institution. These include the National Museum of American History and the National Museum of the American Indian, as well as the

OPPOSITE: THE SCHUYLKILL RIVER
RUNS THROUGH PHILADELPHIA,
PENNSYLVANIA, WHICH WAS THE
COUNTRY'S CAPITAL FROM 1790 TO
1800.
PP. 90-91: THE WHITE HOUSE, THE
PRESIDENT'S OFFICIAL RESIDENCE AND
WORKPLACE, WAS COMPLETED IN
1800.

National Air and Space Museum, where the Apollo Lunar Module and other spacecraft can be examined up-close.

With three large cities that offer so much, the smaller locales in the Mid-Atlantic region risk being overshadowed. Large swaths of New Jersey, Delaware and Maryland are simply residential suburbs of New York, Washington and Philadelphia, but these states are interesting in and of themselves. In the New Jersey town of West Orange, the former house of inventor Thomas Edison has been turned into a museum. Other New Jersey cities include Atlantic City—with a boardwalk and casinos—and Hoboken, where the first game of baseball was played in 1846. The Jersey Shore is a popular summertime beach area.

Delaware—connected to New Jersey via the more than 10,000-foot long Delaware Memorial Bridge—is the second smallest state in the nation, but it, too, offers charming beaches. And the state of Maryland, sandwiched between Pennsylvania and Washington, contains much of the Chesapeake Bay, the largest estuary in the country. The bay is a source of crabs, which are the signature food of the state. Baltimore, Maryland, established in 1729, is a mid-sized city with such landmarks as the Baltimore Basilica, the oldest Catholic cathedral in the United States. Its harbor was

once a major industrial port, but with the fall-off in transportation by water, it fell into disuse. In the 1980s, it was revived with the creation of a large waterfront complex with stores and restaurants, and in 1981 the National Aquarium opened in the area. The aquarium is the city's and the state's biggest most popular attraction. The museum's tanks have the capacity to contain more than 2.2 million gallons of water. Indeed, each area seems almost like a small city of its own.

OPPOSITE: MAYA LIN'S VIETNAM
VETERANS MEMORIAL IN
WASHINGTON, D.C. LISTS THE NAMES
OF MORE THAN 50,000 SOLDIERS
KILLED IN THE WAR.
ABOVE: *THE THREE SOLDIERS* ALSO
PAYS TRIBUTE TO SOLDIERS IN THE
VIETNAM WAR.

MIDWEST

North Dakota

Minnesota

Michigan

Wisconsin

Michigan

South Dakota

Ohio

Iowa

Indiana

Nebraska

Illinois

Missouri

Kansas

MIDWEST

THE PLAINS WHERE PIONEERS STAKED A CLAIM

The Midwest is a set of states whose geography and topography seems to represent their nature. Many of the states in the Midwest are perfectly square, straight lines drawn on a map. The landscape is relatively flat, too, especially on the Great Plains. This is the area of the United States that was settled by European-descended pioneers who traveled westward from the Atlantic coast. Under the various Homestead Acts—the first of which was issued in 1862—settlers could acquire land at little cost. There they planted crops, built houses and created their own communities. These pioneer families lived through difficult times and developed a hardy spirit perhaps best known to modern Americans through *The Little House on the Prairie* and other books by Laura Ingalls Wilder. The Pony Express National Historic Trail, which runs through eight states in the Midwest and the West, still marks the route taken by the precursor to the postal service. These settlers also lived side-by-side with Indians, often encroaching on their ancestral lands, and their presence in the area eventually led to wholesale removal of natives that still has negative repercussions today.

Later, the Midwest would become an area famous for industry—Detroit, Michigan (which, with its notable production of automobiles, earned the nickname Motown, short for Motor Town, which in turn lent its name to Berry Gordy's record company and its famous pop-influenced soul sound), Milwaukee, Wisconsin, and Indianapolis, Indiana were all major manufacturing centers that prospered in the 20th century. Chicago, the largest

city in the Midwest, was aptly termed the "city of the big shoulders" by poet Carl Sandburg. That image of Chicago persists today—a place of burly carnivores and straight talkers—though Chicago is a sophisticated city with spectacular museums, parks and cultural opportunities. (It was also, in the 1920s, home to Al Capone, perhaps the most famous gangster ever to have lived in the United States.)

Indeed, though residents of the two coasts sometimes derisively brush aside the Midwest as a group of "fly-over states," the region has much to offer in terms of culture, architecture, and natural beauty. The Great Lakes are five freshwater lakes (Huron, Ontario, Michigan, Erie and Superior) and numerous smaller bodies of water in the Midwest and Canada (with the exception of Lake Michigan, which is contained within the borders of the United States) that contain 21 percent of the world's fresh surface water and have a total surface area of 94,250 square miles or more than 244,000 square kilometers. Other famed natural sites in this area include the dells of the Wisconsin River with their sandstone rock formations and canyons and soaring cliffs and the many lakes in the state of Minnesota that have earned it the nickname "Land of 10,000 Lakes." Considered in the aggregate, Minnesota's lake shores and riverbanks comprise a larger area than the ocean shorelines of California, Florida and Hawaii.

The state of Michigan is notable for its unusual shape—it looks like a mitten, with another body of land,

known as the Upper Peninsula, to the north of the fingertips. Connecting the two parts of the state is the Mackinac Bridge, opened in 1957. It is the longest suspension bridge in the Western Hemisphere and is 26,372 feet or 8,038 meters long and comprises 42,000 miles (76,592 kilometers) of cable.

One of the most famous attractions in the Midwest is Mount Rushmore, a combination of the manmade and the natural located in the Black Hills of South Dakota and today a national park. Giant busts of four early United States presidents—George Washington, Thomas Jefferson, Theodore Roosevelt and Abraham Lincoln—are carved into the granite face of Mount Rushmore. These likenesses were created in the 1920s and 1930s by a father-son team, Gutzon Borglum and his son, Lincoln Borglum. Today, the area surrounding the monument is a national park that attracts millions of visitors.

Another national park in South Dakota highlights the

ABOVE AND OPPOSITE: DETROIT, MICHIGAN IS HOME TO MANY SKYSCRAPERS.

Badlands, almost 250,000 acres, or close to 100,000 hectares, of grass prairie, buttes, pinnacles and spires in fascinating formations. And Wind Cave National Park in South Dakota is home to bison, elk and prairie dogs, as well as one of the longest caves in the world, known, as its name indicates, for the fierce winds that whip up at its entrance. Underground the cave is articulated into a complex network of "rooms" lined with unique formations called boxwork.

The Midwest was a region with numerous Native American tribes, including the Hurons, the Chippewas, the Lakotas and the Sioux. Naturally, there was tension between all the tribes and European settlers—the first of whom arrived from France in the 17th century. A locus for this conflict was the town of Wounded Knee, located in South Dakota on the Pine Ridge Indian Reservation. In 1890, there had been a shootout between Sioux and the U.S. Army at Wounded Knee when mem-

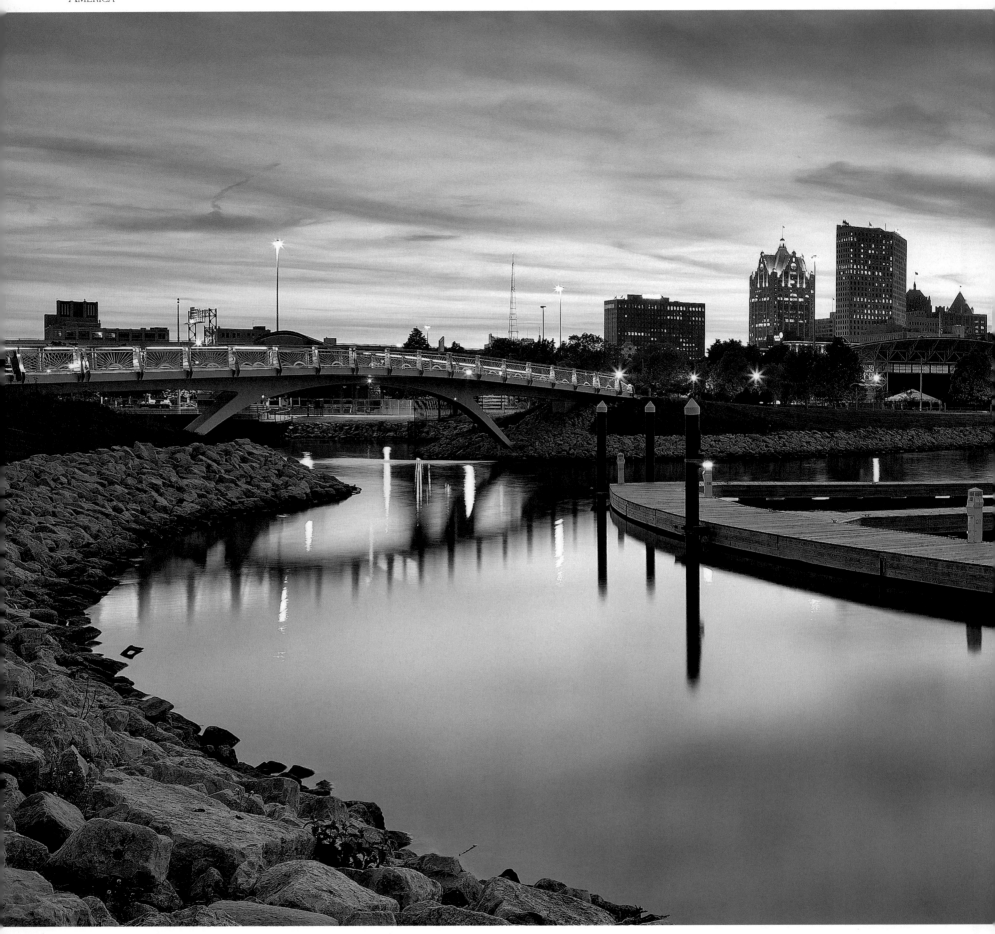

ABOVE: MILWAUKEE, WISCONSIN IS REFLECTED IN LAKE MICHIGAN AS NIGHT FALLS.

bers of the tribe refused to be herded onto reservations. The troops killed hundreds of men, women and children in what is largely considered the last battle in the American Indian Wars.

The Midwest is better known for its wide-open spaces and farmland than it is for museums, yet there is a selection of large and small museums throughout the region that offer interesting perspectives on niche subjects. For example, the Circus World museum is located in Baraboo, Wisconsin, where the Ringling Bros. Circus

PP. 104-105: THE CENTRAL CANAL IN DOWNTOWN INDIANAPOLIS IS LINED WITH A WALKWAY ON EITHER SIDE.
PP. 106-107: STORM CLOUDS GATHER OVER LAKE HURON IN PORT CRESCENT STATE PARK IN MICHIGAN.
PP. 108-109: LAKE MICHIGAN LAPS THE SHORE IN SAUGATUCK DUNES STATE PARK IN MICHIGAN.

was founded in 1884. The site hosts circus performances and also offers exhibits of posters and wooden circus wagons used by traveling circuses. Dearborn, Michigan, a suburb of Detroit, is home to the Arab American National Museum, which exhibits items illustrating Arab-American history, including personal items from famous Arab Americans, like the typewriter used by journalist Helen Thomas in her early career. For its part, Cleveland, Ohio, boasts the Rock & Roll Hall of Fame and Museum, which exhibits everything from Elvis Presley's

ABOVE: THE HISTORIC DELLS MILL
WAS BUILT IN 1864.
OPPOSITE: THIS SANDSTONE
FORMATION IS CHARACTERISTIC OF THE
UNUSUAL SHAPES THAT CAN BE
VIEWED IN THE WISCONSIN RIVER
DELLS.

OPPOSITE: A SHIP PASSES BELOW THE MACKINAC BRIDGE, THE LONGEST SUSPENSION BRIDGE IN THE WESTERN HEMISPHERE.
PP. 114-115: THE FACES OF FOUR PRESIDENTS WERE CARVED INTO MOUNT RUSHMORE IN SOUTH DAKOTA.
PP. 116-117: LIKE MANY MIDWESTERN CITIES, CLEVELAND WAS ONCE AN INDUSTRIAL POWERHOUSE AND HAS REINVENTED ITSELF IN RECENT YEARS.

1975 Lincoln Continental to Jimi Hendrix's handwritten lyrics for "Purple Haze." The Walker Art Center in Minneapolis, Minnesota, focuses on contemporary art and includes a large sculpture garden; Claes Oldenburg and Coosje van Bruggen's *Spoonbridge and Cherry* is its most recognizable piece. In Winterset, Iowa, the John Wayne Birthplace museum celebrates the famous actor.

The Midwest is known as a place of wide open spaces and flat plains, and much of its art and architecture reflect that sense of the local space, which serves as a canvas or backdrop to architectural works. In St. Louis, Missouri, on the border between that state and the state

of Illinois, the renowned Gateway Arch designed by architect Eero Saarinen (who won a competition with this design in 1947) soars over the city. Intended to mark the city as a "gateway to the West," where many settlers passed through on the way to westward expansion, the arch is 630 feet or 192 meters high, as tall as a 63-story building. It is made of 17,246 tons of steel. Visitors can take a tram to the observation deck at the top.

Chicago is a stand-out in this region and has numerous interesting architectural works to visit. Many of Chicago's buildings were constructed in the late 19th and early 20th centuries following a fire that raged

PP. 120-121: EERO SAARINEN'S GATEWAY ARCH IN ST. LOUIS IS THE TALLEST MANMADE MONUMENT IN THE UNITED STATES AND A SYMBOL OF WESTWARD EXPANSION.

across the city in October of 1871 for three days, wiping out more than three square miles (more than nine square kilometers) of the city. (The city was famously roiled again in 1968, not by fire, but by intense political demonstrations when the city played host to the Democratic National Convention.) The Sears Tower was the tallest building in the world when it was completed in 1973 and held that title for more than two decades. The city's Magnificent Mile neighborhood, which runs along Michigan Avenue, is lined with historic buildings in the Beaux Arts and neo-Gothic styles. In the Grant Park neighborhood, the Art Institute of Chicago is a large and

wide-ranging museum established in the 19th century that owns work by everyone from Claude Monet to Pablo Picasso.

Another Chicago landmark is Wrigley Field, the ballpark built in 1914 as the home base for the hard-luck Chicago Cubs. It is the second oldest major league baseball stadium to remain in use; its ivy-covered walls are a signature feature. The Midwest is home to several other unique sporting venues, including the Indianapolis Motor Speedway, where the Indianapolis 500 takes place each year in late May, and horseshoe-shaped Ohio Stadium on the Columbus campus of Ohio State Univer-

119

OPPOSITE: A LION STATUE BY EDWARD
KEMEYS STANDS GUARD OUTSIDE THE
ART INSTITUTE OF CHICAGO.
ABOVE: CHICAGO'S MUSEUM OF
SCIENCE AND INDUSTRY—THE
LARGEST SCIENCE MUSEUM IN THE
WESTERN HEMISPHERE—IS HOUSED
IN A BEAUX ARTS BUILDING THAT WAS
CONSTRUCTED FOR THE WORLD'S
COLUMBIAN EXPOSITION IN 1893.

sity, which seats more than 100,000 and is home to the Ohio State Buckeyes, a football team with a large and fanatical following.

Literature, too, has staked a claim in the Midwest. Iowa City is home to the Iowa Writers' Workshop, the first program in the country to offer a master's degree in creative writing. The workshop has been a training ground for numerous well-known American writers over the years, including John Cheever, Jane Smiley and Philip Roth. Hannibal, Missouri was the hometown of Samuel Clemens, better known by his pen name, Mark Twain. Twain was the author of uniquely American works, including *The Adventures of Tom Sawyer* and *Adven-*

tures of Huckleberry Finn. His home is now a museum open to the public. And while L. Frank Baum was not a native of the Midwest, he set his book *The Wonderful Wizard of Oz* in Kansas. The book has been adapted many times over the years and is perhaps best remembered in the form of the 1939 film *The Wizard of Oz*, starring Judy Garland as Dorothy, who is lifted by a tornado from her family's farm and lands in a fantasy world, where she turns to her dog and famously says, "I've got a feeling we're not in Kansas anymore." Kansas today hosts an Oz Museum that contains memorabilia from books and movies.

ABOVE: CHICAGO'S SKYSCRAPERS RUN ALONGSIDE LAKE MICHIGAN.
OPPOSITE: THE WILLIS TOWER (MORE COMMONLY KNOWN AS THE SEARS TOWER), SEEN HERE IN THE CENTER OF A VIEW OF THE CHICAGO SKYLINE, WAS THE TALLEST BUILDING IN THE WORLD WHEN IT WAS COMPLETED IN 1973.
PP. 126-127: THE STAINLESS STEEL *CLOUD GATE* BY ANISH KAPOOR REFLECTS ITS SURROUNDINGS IN MILLENNIUM PARK IN CHICAGO.

OPPOSITE: SOLDIER FIELD IN
CHICAGO—WHERE THE CHICAGO
BEARS PLAY—HOSTED ITS FIRST
FOOTBALL GAME IN 1924.

TOM SAWYER'S FENCE
HERE STOOD THE BOARD
FENCE WHICH TOM SAWYER
PERSUADED HIS GANG TO
PAY HIM FOR THE PRIVILEGE
OF WHITEWASHING. TOM
SAT BY AND SAW THAT IT
WAS WELL DONE.

OPPOSITE: WRITER MARK TWAIN'S
BOYHOOD HOME IN HANNIBAL, MISSOURI
IS NOW A MUSEUM. TWAIN, BORN SAMUEL
CLEMENS, WROTE THE QUINTESSENTIAL
AMERICAN NOVELS *THE ADVENTURES OF
TOM SAWYER* AND *ADVENTURES OF
HUCKLEBERRY FINN.*

SOUTH

West Virginia

Virginia

Kentucky

North Carolina

Tennessee

South Carolina

Oklahoma

Arkansas

Georgia

Alabama

Mississippi

Florida

Texas

Louisiana

SOUTH

MILD CLIMES AND A SLOWER PACE

The South of the United States is generally defined as the states that were part of or allied with the Confederacy that attempted to secede from the North, known as the Union, during the American Civil War in the 1860s. This area maintains a unique culture and in some ways has fiercely resisted blending with the rest of the country. While modern life and the lightning-speed communication afforded by the Internet have smoothed over the regional differences in the United States, mellowing accents and replacing traditional local foods with more generic choices, the residents of the South have clung to their history with particular fierceness. Perhaps it's the warmer climate of the South, the slower speech patterns, the more conservative politics, or the area's agricultural past—though the South these days is home to the headquarters of giant corporations, such as Coca-Cola in Atlanta, Georgia—or some combination of the above that causes this region to keep to itself more than others.

While race is an issue throughout the United States—throughout the world, even—the South was the site where battles were fought in the 1950s and 1960s to eliminate segregation in schools and public spaces. Prior to that, under so-called "Jim Crow" laws, people of color were often relegated to separate schools, bathrooms, drinking fountains, waiting rooms, and buses and train cars in the South and in some other areas of the country. Because segregation was so much more rigidly enforced there (though there were segregated places in the North

as well, segregation was never as institutionalized), the protests and marches and legal cases that eventually culminated in greater equality were located in the South as well.

On December 1, 1955 in Montgomery, Alabama, a department store seamstress named Rosa Parks boarded a bus to go home. At the time, there was a demarcation in that city's buses: African-American passengers were required to pay their fare at the front, where the driver sat, then exit the bus and enter through the rear door. If the space initially allotted to white passengers in the front became crowded, the driver would move the line back, taking seats from African-American passengers and giving them to white passengers. On that day in December, the line was shifted, but Rosa Parks—seated in what had been the front of the African-American section—refused to move.

Her subsequent arrest led to a boycott of the bus system that lasted for more than a year and successfully ended segregation of the bus system, and in wider terms, it began a revolution. Baptist minister Martin Luther King, Jr. was one of the organizers of the boycott, and earned national attention as a civil rights leader for the first time. King, a native of Georgia, would go on to lead the March on Washington in 1963 that led directly to passage of the Civil Rights Act in 1964. Today, there is a National Historic Site dedicated to him that includes the home in Atlanta where he was born, the church where he served as minister, and the King Center, which has ex-

OPPOSITE: A STATUE OF LONGTIME
SENATOR AND ARCH-CONSERVATIVE
STROM THURMOND STANDS OUTSIDE
THE SOUTH CAROLINA STATE CAPITOL
BUILDING.
ABOVE: STONE MOUNTAIN PARK IN
GEORGIA, THE SOUTH'S ANSWER TO
MOUNT RUSHMORE, DEPICTS
CONFEDERATE ARMY GENERALS.

hibits on his life and on peace activism and is also the location of his tomb. Montgomery is home to the Civil Rights Memorial, a Maya Lin monument that lists the names of 40 people who died in the struggle between 1954 and 1968. There is also a marker on the spot where Rosa Parks boarded that fateful bus in Montgomery, and a more recent memorial to her (Parks passed away in 2005) that reads "She sat down, so we can stand up."

This rather serious introduction to the American South may leave a mistaken impression of this area of the United States. The South is also a place known for

revelry. In Kentucky, the Kentucky Derby is an annual horse-racing that features not just the athleticism of animals and jockeys, but also lavish parties, women in royal wedding-worthy hats and mint juleps (bourbon cocktails).

The area outside of Orlando, Florida is home to Disney World, the most visited entertainment site in the world. The resort opened in 1971. Far more than a mere theme park, it is about twice the size of Manhattan and employs more than 60,000 people. Main Street, USA, the faux small-town boulevard that runs through the

ABOVE: THIS ILLUSTRATION DEPICTS THE UNION ARMY (REPRESENTING THE NORTH) BOMBING OF FORT SUMTER IN CHARLESTON, SOUTH CAROLINA, CONSIDERED THE BIRTHPLACE OF THE CIVIL WAR.
OPPOSITE: THIS RESIDENCE IS PART OF THE OFFICERS' QUARTERS AT FORT MCALLISTER, BUILT IN THE EARLY 1800S NEAR SAVANNAH, GEORGIA.

center of the park, was modeled after the central street in Marceline, Missouri, where Walt Disney spent his childhood. Though the park was a long-nurtured dream of his, he passed away before it opened.

Elsewhere in Florida, the art deco architecture in Miami's South Beach neighborhood is not only stunning in its own right, but has spurred the creation of a more adult vacation destination. Miami is only about 230 miles (370 kilometers) from the city of Havana and has absorbed a large number of Cuban immigrants over the years. The Little Havana neighborhood of Miami centers

around SW 8th Street, known as Calle Ocho. Here, the many Cuban restaurants and the Cuban-style street life recreate the atmosphere of the island, and the Calle Ocho Walk of Fame, modeled on the Hollywood Walk of Fame, celebrates local Latinos.

The Mardi Gras celebrations in New Orleans, Louisiana, are some of the most festive in the world. The city is transformed during the Carnival season by parades with massive floats, colorful costumes, and bands performing local music. It was the French settlers in Louisiana who began the tradition of raucous Mardi

REV. MARTIN LUTHER KING, JR.
1929—1968

Free at last. Free at last.
Thank God Almighty
I'm Free at last.

OPPOSITE: THE GRANITE MARTIN LUTHER KING, JR. MEMORIAL, HONORING THE GEORGIA NATIVE, IS LOCATED IN WASHINGTON, D.C. IN 1963, KING LED THE FAMOUS MARCH ON WASHINGTON SEEKING CIVIL RIGHTS. HE GAVE HIS MOST FAMOUS SPEECH, "I HAVE A DREAM," ON THAT OCCASION.
ABOVE: THE MARTIN LUTHER KING, JR. NATIONAL HISTORIC SITE IS LOCATED IN ATLANTA, GEORGIA AND INCORPORATES BOTH A MEMORIAL AND A CENTER FOR NONVIOLENT SOCIAL CHANGE. KING AND HIS WIFE, CORETTA SCOTT KING, ARE INTERRED THERE.

Gras celebrations. The parades date back to the 1800s and are run by neighborhood groups that compete to see who can offer the most elaborate constructions. All of Louisiana bears the marks of Cajun and Creole cultures, a local outgrowth of French settlers (via Canada in the case of Cajuns). Another local hallmark is voodoo, a spiritual system with roots in Africa. The New Orleans Historic Voodoo Museum not only houses exhibits on the subject and features information about Marie Laveau, known as the Voodoo Queen of New Orleans, but also organizes walking tours.

New Orleans—which is tamer, but by no means tame the rest of the year—is also known for zydeco and Dixieland jazz, and music is an important component in southern culture in general. Beale Street in Memphis, Tennessee is lined with blues clubs where the musical style known as Memphis blues evolved in the hands of musicians like B.B. King and Muddy Waters. Memphis is also home to Graceland, the over-the-top estate of Elvis Presley. Today, the home is a museum. (Presley's birthplace in Tupelo, Mississippi is also open to visitors.) Elsewhere in Tennessee, Nashville's Grand Ole Opry, a weekly country music concert, is still staged. Originating as a radio show in 1925, the Grand Ole Opry pop-

141

...UNTIL JUSTICE ROLLS DOWN LIKE WATERS
AND RIGHTEOUSNESS LIKE A MIGHTY STREAM

MARTIN LUTHER KING, JR.

28 AUG 1955 EMMETT LO...
SPEAKING TO...

13 AUG 1955 LAMAR SMITH MUR...
BLACK VOTERS BROO...

7 MAY 1955 REV GEORGE LEE KILLE...
VOTER REGISTRATION DR...

17 MAY 1954 SUPREME COURT OUTLAW...
SEGREGATION IN BROWN...
OF EDUCATION

4 APR 1968 DR. MARTIN LUTHER KING JR.
ASSASSINATED MEMPHIS, TN

Eighty-eighth Congress of the United States of America

AT THE SECOND SESSION

Begun and held at the City of Washington on Tuesday, the seventh day of January, one thousand nine hundred and sixty-four

An Act

To enforce the constitutional right to vote, to confer jurisdiction upon the district courts of the United States to provide injunctive relief against discrimination in public accommodations, to authorize the Attorney General to institute suits to protect constitutional rights in public facilities and public education, to extend the Commission on Civil Rights, to prevent discrimination in federally assisted programs, to establish a Commission on Equal Employment Opportunity, and for other purposes.

Be it enacted by the Senate and House of Representatives of the United States of America in Congress assembled, That this Act may be cited as the "Civil Rights Act of 1964".

TITLE I—VOTING RIGHTS

SEC. 101. Section 2004 of the Revised Statutes (42 U.S.C. 1971), as amended by section 131 of the Civil Rights Act of 1957 (71 Stat. 637), and as further amended by section 601 of the Civil Rights Act of 1960 (74 Stat. 90), is further amended as follows:

(a) Insert "1" after "(a)" in subsection (a) and add at the end of subsection (a) the following new paragraphs:

"(2) No person acting under color of law shall—

"(A) in determining whether any individual is qualified under State law or laws to vote in any Federal election, apply any standard, practice, or procedure different from the standards, practices, or procedures applied under such law or laws to other individuals within the same county, parish, or similar political subdivision who have been found by State officials to be qualified to vote;

"(B) deny the right of any individual to vote in any Federal election because of an error or omission on any record or paper relating to any application, registration, or other act requisite to voting, if such error or omission is not material in determining whether such individual is qualified under State law to vote in such election; or

"(C) employ any literacy test as a qualification for voting in any Federal election unless (i) such test is administered to each individual and is conducted wholly in writing, and (ii) a certified copy of the test and of the answers given by the individual is furnished to him within twenty-five days of the submission of his request made within the period of time during which records and papers are required to be retained and preserved pursuant to title III of the Civil Rights Act of 1960 (42 U.S.C. 1974–74e; 74 Stat. 88): *Provided, however,* That the Attorney General may enter into agreements with appropriate State or local authorities that preparation, conduct, and maintenance of such tests in accordance with the provisions of applicable State or local law, including such special provisions as are necessary in the preparation, conduct, and maintenance of such tests for persons who are blind or otherwise physically handicapped, meet the purposes of this subparagraph and constitute compliance therewith.

"(3) For purposes of this subsection—

"(A) the term 'vote' shall have the same meaning as in subsection (e) of this section;

"(B) the phrase 'literacy test' includes any test of the ability to read, write, understand, or interpret any matter."

(b) Insert immediately following the period at the end of the first sentence of subsection (c) the following new sentence: "If in any such proceeding literacy is a relevant fact there shall be a rebuttable

ularized country music performers such as Patsy Cline and Hank Williams.

Other charming small cities in the South include Charlottesville, Virginia (where Monticello, the gracious home of Thomas Jefferson, the country's third president, and now a UNESCO World Heritage Site is located),

OPPOSITE: MIAMI BEACH, FLORIDA IS KNOWN FOR NIGHTLIFE AND PRISTINE BEACHES.
ABOVE: OCEAN DRIVE IN MIAMI'S SOUTH BEACH NEIGHBORHOOD IS LINED WITH BEAUTIFULLY RESTORED ART DECO HOTELS.

145

OPPOSITE: IN NEW ORLEANS, A MULE
PULLS A CARRIAGE THROUGH THE
STREETS.

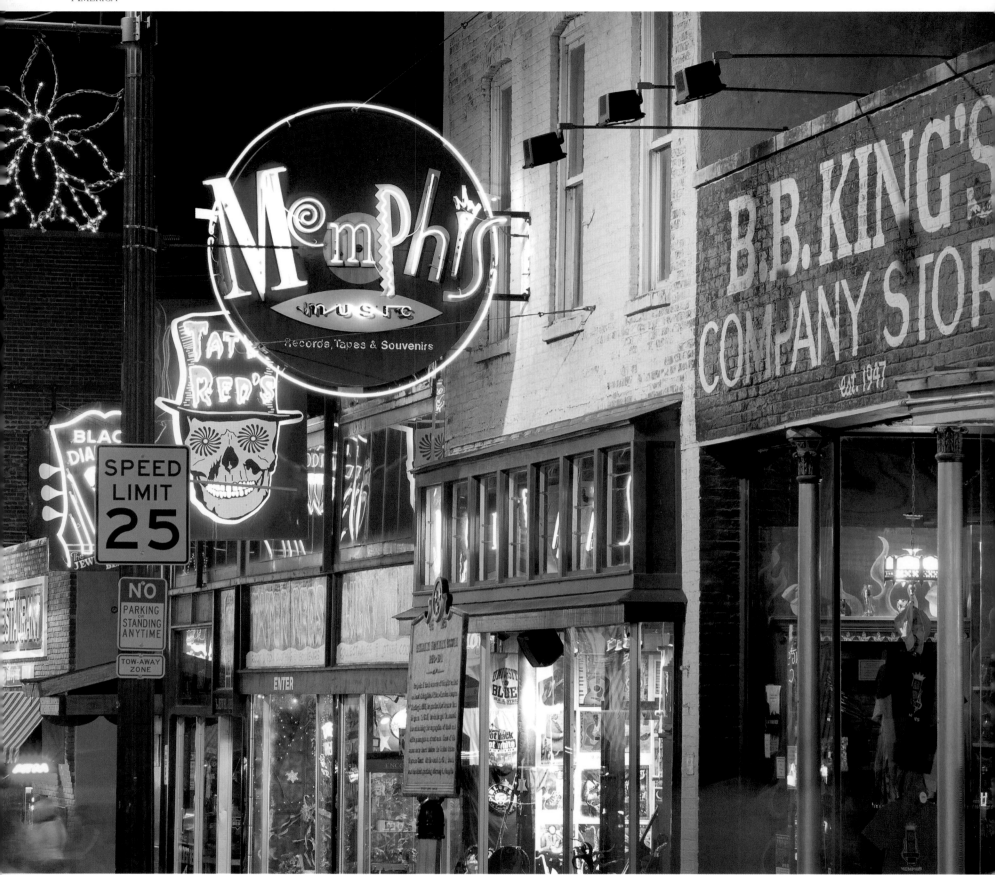

ABOVE: BLUES CLUBS ON HISTORIC
BEALE STREET IN MEMPHIS,
TENNESSEE COMPETE FOR CUSTOMERS
WITH NEON SIGNS.
OPPOSITE: A STATUE OF ELVIS
PRESLEY STRIKES A SOULFUL POSE ON
BEALE STREET.

Charleston, South Carolina and Savannah, Georgia, with its 22 lovely squares, each of which is the centerpiece of a different neighborhood.

And then there's the state that's anything but small and charming: Texas. The largest of the 48 contiguous states in the United States (Alaska is larger) and bigger than the country of France, Texas is known as a brash place of outsized personalities, cities full of skyscrapers, and a culture of confidence—some might say braggadocio. Oil was first discovered in Texas in 1901, and that discovery has had great impact on the state's culture, as well as its finances. The state rode a massive oil boom for many years, and oil money fueled quick growth in

the cities of Houston and Dallas. Downtown Houston has towering buildings such as One Shell Plaza (the tallest in the city when completed in 1971) and Pennzoil Place (1975) by Philip Johnson and John Burgee. The Bank of America Plaza in downtown Dallas is 72 stories high. Its perimeter is lined with argon tube lights that shine green against the night sky. Outside of its cities, Texas is also very actively agricultural and has a long history of ranching. The National Cowgirl Museum and Hall of Fame in Fort Worth, Texas specifically honors the women who once rode the range.

The South has no shortage of beautiful natural environments, either. The Outer Banks are a series of islands

OPPOSITE: THE UNIVERSITY OF VIRGINIA IN CHARLOTTESVILLE, VIRGINIA WAS DESIGNED BY THOMAS JEFFERSON AND FOUNDED IN 1819.
ABOVE: THE HISTORIC CHARLESTON FOUNDATION, HEADQUARTERED IN THIS BRICK BUILDING, IS DEDICATED TO PRESERVING AND HIGHLIGHTING THE ARCHITECTURE OF CHARLESTON, SOUTH CAROLINA.

off the coast of North Carolina that include the town of Kitty Hawk, where the Wright brothers first flew an airplane. (Today the Wright Brothers National Memorial marks the spot.) In South Carolina, Hilton Head Island is a pleasant resort destination famous for its golf courses. The Ozark Mountains roll gently across Oklahoma, Missouri and Arkansas. And the Florida Keys, an archipelago that sits southwest of mainland Florida, are known for their laid-back style and tropical beaches. Connecting the various islands in the Keys is the Seven Mile Bridge. Key West was home to famous American writer Ernest Hemingway, whose house is a popular tourist attraction. The feline descendants of Hemingway's cat roam the grounds—they are famously poly-

dactyl, with extra "toes" on their paws. The southernmost point in the continental United States is located on the island of Key West and marked by a concrete buoy, and every evening people gather in Mallory Square on Key West to watch the sun drop below the horizon, another of the South's treasured traditions.

OPPOSITE: SAVANNAH, GEORGIA HAS MORE THAN ITS SHARE OF GRACEFUL ARCHITECTURE, INCLUDING ITS GLEAMING CITY HALL.
ABOVE: THIS IS ONE OF HUNDREDS OF LOVELY BUILDINGS THAT SURROUND SAVANNAH'S 22 SQUARES.

OPPOSITE: THE BUILDINGS IN THE HOUSTON, TEXAS SKYLINE SEEM TO REACH FOR THE CLOUDS.
ABOVE: OIL RIGS LOOK LIKE LARGE-SCALE SCULPTURES AGAINST THE TEXAS SKY.

OPPOSITE: THE DALLAS SKYLINE
INCLUDES THE REUNION TOWER, AN
OBSERVATION DECK (SHOWN HERE ON
THE LEFT), AND THE SHARPLY ANGLED
FOUNTAIN PLACE (CENTER).

ABOVE: THE WRIGHT BROTHERS NATIONAL MEMORIAL COMMEMORATES THE FIRST AIRPLANE FLIGHT NEAR KITTY HAWK IN NORTH CAROLINA.
OPPOSITE: BROTHERS AND AIR TRAVEL INNOVATORS WILBUR AND ORVILLE WRIGHT ARE HONORED WITH A 60-FOOT TALL GRANITE MONUMENT IN KITTY HAWK.

OPPOSITE: THE HARBOUR TOWN
LIGHTHOUSE ON HILTON HEAD,
SOUTH CAROLINA WEARS JAUNTY
RED-AND-WHITE STRIPES.
ABOVE: ERNEST HEMINGWAY LIVED
ON THE ISLAND OF KEY WEST FOR
MORE THAN 10 YEARS. POLYDACTYL
(SIX-TOED) CATS STILL ROAM THE
GROUNDS OF HIS FORMER HOME—
MANY ARE DESCENDANTS OF A
SIX-TOED CAT HEMINGWAY KEPT AS A
PET.

MOUNTAIN
WEST

Montana

Idaho

Wyoming

Nevada

Utah

Colorado

Arizona

New Mexico

MOUNTAIN WEST

CANYONS, MOUNTAINS AND DRAMATIC DESERT

The Mountain West region of the United States is wildly diverse and endlessly fascinating. It encompasses eight different states and impressive natural features—soaring mountains, deep canyons, seemingly endless desert. Buttes and forests abound. But the American West is more than a mere place; it is also an ideal, and it holds a unique position in the world's imagination as a frontier, a "wild" place, and an area of open skies (the state of Montana is nicknamed "Big Sky Country") and open spaces. The setting of countless movies—so many that Westerns form a film genre of their own—the West is perhaps the most uniquely American part of the United States. As Pulitzer Prize-winning writer Wallace Stegner, who chronicled life in the West in both his fiction and his non-fiction, once said, "The West is America, only more so."

It's interesting to note, then, that the definition of "the West" has shifted drastically over time. Initially, the phrase "the West" indicated all of mainland America west of the Mississippi River. As those areas were developed, they no longer meshed with the image of the West in the popular imagination (think John Wayne movies) and they were shifted, at least psychologically, to the Midwest.

The Mountain West, too, was home to Native Americans and was the site of slaughter, displacement and mistreatment as European settlers pushed westward. Wars and lesser conflicts raged in this area for decades, and the relocation of large groups of indigenous people remains an unresolved and in many ways unexplored national embarrassment. Native Americans were often forced to walk for miles; many died from illness and exposure. The legacy of these conflicts, which lasted until the early 1900s, can still be felt today. That said, there are many interesting native sites in the region. Medicine Wheel, a national historic landmark in Wyoming, is a well-preserved Crow ceremonial site. Aztec Ruins National Monument in northwestern New Mexico offers the ruins of Indian (though not Aztec—the name is a misnomer) pueblo buildings from close to a millennium ago and is a UNESCO World Heritage Site.

While most other areas of the country are defined largely by their cities, with development expanding outward from them in concentric circles, the West's most recognizable locales are natural. (And the cities that are famous in this region are on the small side and associated with natural features, such as beautiful Aspen, Colorado, a former mining town and now a skier's paradise tucked high in the Rocky Mountains, or equally charming Taos, New Mexico, with its challenging trails. Santa Fe, New Mexico is the highest-elevation state capital in the country at 7,199 feet above sea level and is home to the Georgia O'Keefe Museum.) This area hosts the most celebrated national parks in the United States, the protected areas championed vociferously by Theodore Roosevelt (a conservationist and nature lover who, though born and raised

163

OPPOSITE: NATIVE AMERICAN
CULTURE IS STILL PRESERVED IN MANY
PARTS OF THE WEST AND ELSEWHERE
IN THE UNITED STATES.
ABOVE: OLD WOODEN WAGONS
POPULATE THE STREETS OF A GHOST
TOWN IN CODY, WYOMING.

OPPOSITE: TAOS PUEBLO IN NEW
MEXICO SITS IN A SPECTACULAR
NATURAL SETTING; THE COMMUNITY
HAS BEEN INHABITED FOR MORE THAN
1,000 YEARS.
ABOVE: AZTEC RUINS NATIONAL
MONUMENT IN NEW MEXICO IS ALSO
HOME TO PUEBLO BUILDINGS (THOUGH
NOT AZTEC) THAT DATE BACK MORE
THAN A MILLENNIUM.

Opposite: Tiny Ouray, Colorado nestles in the Rocky Mountains. It was originally a mining town. **pp. 170-171:** The Teton mountain range, a sub-section of the Rocky Mountains, offers spectacular scenery.

in New York City, loved the American West) during his presidency from 1901 to 1909.

Yellowstone National Park sits largely in Wyoming, but parts of it cross into Montana and Idaho. The world's first national park, it was established in 1872. Yellowstone, a gigantic 3,472 square miles (8,987 square kilometers) in size is home to numerous geysers, including Old Faithful, which erupts every 35 minutes to two hours as regularly as any automated system (hence its name). The park as a whole is home to the largest group of geysers, hot springs, mudpots and fumaroles on the planet—a full half of the world's hydrothermal features. It is also home to a large wildlife population, including bears, bison, 330 different species of birds, and wolves. In the face of declining populations, gray wolves were reintroduced to the park in the 1990s.

Yellowstone attracts more than three million visitors annually, a significant number, but Grand Canyon National Park in Arizona is even more popular, drawing nearly five million people a year to stand on the rim of its one-mile (1.6-kilometer) deep canyon and peer into the abyss. The canyon, carved by the Colorado River as it wore through layers of rock, is 18 miles wide at its widest point. It is truly an awesome sight .

These are just two of the better known national parks. Smaller (yet still large by most standards) parks include Glacier National Park in Montana with its

mountains and lakes. The park is home to wolves, bears, wolverines and lynx, and it is crisscrossed by more than 740 miles (1,190 kilometers) of hiking trails. In the state of Utah, Bryce Canyon National Park (a series of natural "amphitheaters" eroded into a plateau), Zion National Park (filled with jagged red and pink sandstone cliffs) and Arches National Park (with more than 2,000 natural rock arches and other fascinating formations) each has its own flavor, as do Utah's Monument Valley with its sandstone buttes and Colorado's Rattlesnake Canyon with its quirky natural arches and the 535-million-year-old Chimney Rock in Colorado. Red Rocks in Colorado boasts numerous red sandstone formations. Carlsbad Caverns in New Mexico includes a natural limestone "room" that is almost 4,000 feet long. It is the seventh largest such space in the world. The stalactites grow to enormous length and resemble willow trees.

These rock formation are impressive, but they are dwarfed by the massive mountains that fill this region. The Rocky Mountains (aka the Rockies) run from Canada down into the United States and cut across the states of Montana, Idaho, Wyoming, Colorado, Utah and New Mexico, but it is Colorado that is perhaps most closely associated with this 3,000-mile (4,800-kilometer) long range. The Teton mountain range (whose peaks are also largely preserved as a national park) is a sub-section of the Rocky Mountains. Wyoming's Big Horn Mountains are a sister range to

OPPOSITE: ASPEN, COLORADO, ONCE A MINING CAMP, OFFERS CHALLENGING SLOPES AND OTHER OPPORTUNITIES FOR OUTDOOR RECREATION.
PP. 174-175: THE GRAND PRISMATIC SPRING IN YELLOWSTONE NATIONAL PARK IS THE LARGEST HOT SPRING IN THE UNITED STATES. GEOLOGISTS NOTED ITS BRILLIANT RAINBOW HUES AS EARLY AS 1871.

OPPOSITE: YELLOWSTONE NATIONAL PARK, THE WORLD'S FIRST NATIONAL PARK, WAS ESTABLISHED IN 1872. ITS 3,472 SQUARE MILES (8,987 KILOMETERS) ARE HOME TO AN ALMOST INFINITE NUMBER OF NATURAL PHENOMENA, INCLUDING THIS GRACEFUL WATERFALL THROUGH A CANYON.
ABOVE: A BISON GRAZES AGAINST THE BACKDROP OF AN ERUPTING OLD FAITHFUL GEYSER IN YELLOWSTONE NATIONAL PARK.

the Rocky Mountains and are home to a national forest. The mountainous continental divide of the Americas cuts through this region of the Untied States.

Looking at a topographical map, it almost seems that any part of the Mountain West that isn't mountainous is desert. Parts of the Mojave Desert and the Sonoran Desert with its bristly saguaro cactuses (the namesakes to Arizona's Saguaro National Park) cross broad swaths of the region, particularly its southern part.

Culturally, the Mountain West is a hub for outdoor activities—skiing, camping, hiking, bicycling and many other recreational activities are widely enjoyed in the region. The area also includes two diametrically opposed places, culturally speaking: freewheeling Nevada and buttoned up Utah. Nevada is the only state in the United States where gambling is legal. (It is legal in isolated areas of other states.) Las Vegas, Nevada is known

for its casinos and its freewheeling nightlife. The "strip" that runs through the center of Las Vegas is lined on either side with flashy, larger-than-life themed casinos where high rollers play roulette, baccarat, blackjack and more. Prostitution is also legal in many parts of Nevada, and the state has very lenient laws about both marriage and divorce, with no waiting period for a marriage license. This has led to such institutions as drive-through chapels for quick weddings. The Burlesque Hall of Fame in Las Vegas celebrates the kind of lascivious entertainment that in the pre-Internet age especially was much sought out in Las Vegas.

Utah, on the other hand, is a state that is largely controlled by Mormons, members of a religion that originated in upstate New York. In 1844, leader Brigham Young moved the church from New York to Utah, which was sparsely populated at the time (and where members of the sect could practice polygamy in

OPPOSITE: THE GRAND CANYON,
CARVED THROUGH ROCK BY THE
COLORADO RIVER, IS 18 MILES WIDE
AT ITS WIDEST POINT.
ABOVE: THE COLORADO RIVER
WENDS ITS WAY THROUGH A TYPICAL
WESTERN LANDSCAPE.
PP. 180-181: GLACIER NATIONAL
PARK IS A SERENE PLACE FILLED WITH
NATURAL WONDERS AND A WIDE
VARIETY OF ANIMAL SPECIES.

ABOVE: THOR'S HAMMER IN BRYCE
CANYON NATIONAL PARK SEEMS TO
TEETER PRECARIOUSLY. THE ROCK
FORMATIONS IN THE CANYON ARE
KNOWN AS "HOODOOS."
OPPOSITE: ZION NATIONAL PARK IN
UTAH IS FILLED WITH JAGGED RED
AND PINK SANDSTONE FORMATIONS.

182

ABOVE: ONE OF THE MORE THAN 2,000 NATURAL ARCHES IN ARCHES NATIONAL PARK GLOWS ORANGE IN THE SUN.
OPPOSITE: HUNTS MESA IN MONUMENT VALLEY OFFERS STRIKING VIEWS.
PP. 186-187: SANDSTONE PILLARS STAND LIKE SENTRIES IN MONUMENT VALLEY.

OPPOSITE: CHIMNEY PEAK SERVES AS A BACKDROP FOR ASPENS IN COLORADO'S UNCOMPAHGRE NATIONAL FOREST.

OPPOSITE: THE WAVE, A STRIKING
SANDSTONE FORMATION IN ARIZONA,
TRULY APPEARS TO MOVE.
ABOVE: THE RED ROCKS IN
ARIZONA'S HIGH DESERT ARE A
FAVORITE FOR HIKING.
PP. 192-193: DESPITE THE HIGH
TEMPERATURES THE SONORAN DESERT
EXPERIENCES, IT IS SURPRISINGLY
VERDANT.

peace), and today more than 60 percent of the state's population is Mormon. In Salt Lake City, Mormons built the spiky Salt Lake Temple, which was opened in 1893. Because of the Mormon influence in Salt Lake City, the sale of alcohol is highly restricted. Even coffee and cola can be hard to locate, because Mormons are forbidden to ingest caffeine. It's an exaggeration to say that all of Utah is like this—Park City, Utah, for example, is home to the Sundance Film Festival, an annual indie, largely leftist celebration of cinema—but there is certainly a more somber tone to life in this state.

OPPOSITE: THE LAS VEGAS STRIP LIGHTS UP EVERY NIGHT.
ABOVE: THE LAS VEGAS STRIP IS LINED WITH CASINOS.

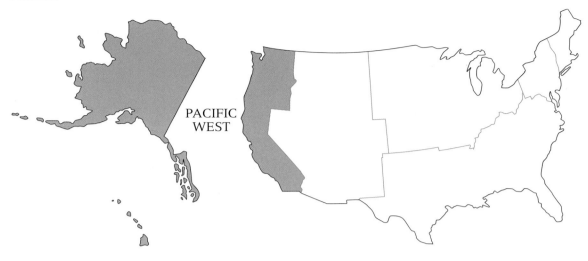

PACIFIC
WEST

Alaska

Hawaii

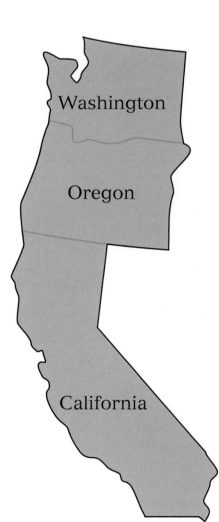

Washington

Oregon

California

PACIFIC WEST

PALM TREES AND REDWOODS, PLUS THE COUNTRY'S MOST RECENT ADDITIONS

The Pacific West, the region of the United States consisting of the three contiguous states along the coast of the Pacific Ocean, plus Alaska and Hawaii, is an area full of dramatic natural scenery. California—the most populous state in the United States and one of the largest—runs along the Pacific coastline and has often been at the forefront of cultural shifts around the world. It is the home of Hollywood, the birthplace of the hippie movement and a spot perpetually linked to change, evolution and starting over.

California stretches 840 miles along the Pacific coast and was granted statehood in 1850, two years after gold had been discovered there. From 1848 to 1855, the state was flooded with prospectors—it's estimated that 300,000 people came to mine for gold, most of them in 1849. (The San Francisco football team, the 49ers, are named after the gold miners.) This influx of people—and the wealth that resulted from gold when it was found—had tremendous impact, and California evolved quickly from an isolated place cut off from the rest of the country by the Sierra Nevada Mountains to a booming state. San Francisco developed from a tiny settlement to a full-fledged city in less than a decade.

San Francisco remains one of the loveliest cities in the United States today. Perhaps its best-known landmark is the Golden Gate Bridge, a long suspension bridge across the bay that is often partially eclipsed by San Francisco's famous fog. The city also has a network of cable cars that bounce up and down its rolling hills.

During the so-called "Summer of Love," the summer of 1967, people seeking to get involved in the burgeoning hippie counterculture flooded the city's Haight-Ashbury district with its ramshackle Victorian houses. The Castro neighborhood of San Francisco was the site of a different revolution: It was one of the first recognizably gay neighborhoods in the United States and remains an epicenter of the LGBT civil rights struggle today. San Francisco's Chinatown neighborhood has the largest population of Chinese people outside of China itself. Alcatraz Island is located in the city's bay and is the site of Alcatraz Federal Penitentiary, which today is a historical site, but was once a prison considered inescapable.

San Francisco may be a bustling city today, but it is still dwarfed by California's other city: Los Angeles. The country's second most populous city, Los Angeles sprawls across Southern California. It is a city that grows wider, but not too tall—this city sits on several faults, including the San Andreas Fault, making it prone to earthquakes.

Los Angeles consists of many different neighborhoods, but there is one whose name is indelibly linked with it: Hollywood. Hollywood is specifically a neighborhood in Los Angeles, but it is also used as a catchall phrase for American moviemaking, and for a certain type of glamour. In many ways, the exceedingly pleasant climate of Los Angeles shaped the city's destiny. The year-round warm and sunny weather in Southern California drew many film productions to the area. (The mild local

PP. 200-201: CHARMING VICTORIAN HOUSES LINE ALAMO SQUARE IN SAN FRANCISCO. THE CITY'S SKYLINE LOOMS BEHIND THEM.

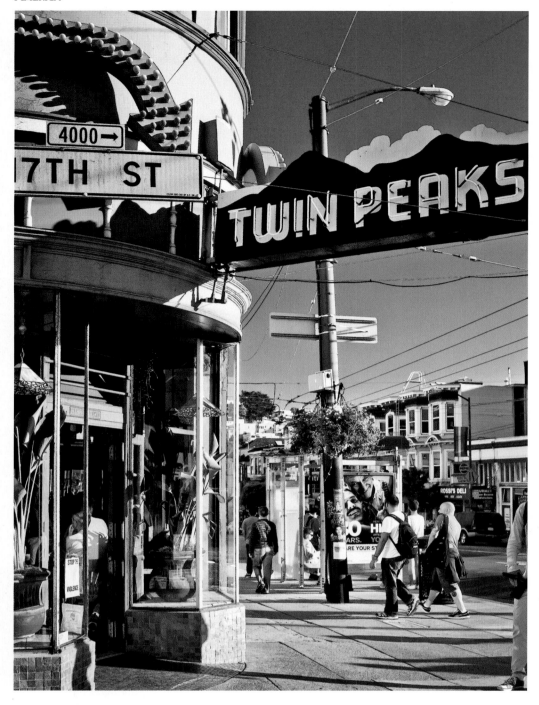

climate also encouraged creation of the Hollywood Bowl, an open-air theater built in 1926 and based on ancient Greek and Roman amphitheaters.) By the 1920s, the Hollywood neighborhood was established as an area for movie studios, though one of its most recognizable buildings is linked not to film, but to music—the Capitol Records Tower, which resembles a stack of records stacked on top of each other, was completed in 1956. That building sits near the corner of Hollywood Boulevard and Vine Street, once considered the epicenter of the movie industry and, at least apocryphally, a spot where aspiring starlets stood if they wished to be discovered. Further along on Hollywood Boulevard stands Grauman's Chinese Theater, a cartoonishly "Asian-style" movie theater built in the 1920s. Since that time, it has been traditional for stars to set their handprints and signatures in the wet cement of the concrete in front of the theater before it dries. The Hollywood Walk of Fame on the same street features stars set into the sidewalk with famous names across them. On the hills above Hollywood is the famous Hollywood sign, whose white block letters were initially erected in 1923 as part of an advertising campaign for a housing development called "Hollywoodland."

Though it can be hard for visitors to spend time indoors when the beaches of Santa Monica, Malibu and Venice (which, like its Italian namesake, has a series of canals) are calling, Los Angeles also has several notable art museums. The Los Angeles County Museum of Art

OPPOSITE: SAN FRANCISCO IS FAMOUS FOR ITS GOLDEN GATE BRIDGE—AND EQUALLY FAMOUS FOR ITS THICK FOG.
PP. 206-207: THE HOLLYWOOD SIGN HAS COME TO SYMBOLIZE MOVIEMAKING AND GLAMOUR, BUT IT WAS ORIGINALLY ERECTED IN 1923 AS AN ADVERTISEMENT FOR A HOUSING DEVELOPMENT.

So DEAR – MY WISH
IS FOR YOUR SUCCESS
Norma Talmadge
MAY 18
1927

᙭ O'TOOLE
᙭-4-11

AUG-7-1941
HAND and BooT Prints

Good luck Sid.

Douglas Fairbanks

HAnd and FooT Prints

"Will Smith
Change the World"
12.10.07

(known as LACMA) owns a broad collection that includes more than 100,000 objects housed in seven buildings. The collection includes work by René Magritte and Frida Kahlo, and the museum also boasts a large collection of California Arts and Crafts furniture and housewares. The Getty Museum has two locations: The Getty Center in the city of Los Angeles contains mostly European and American art, while the Getty Villa perches in a fabulous position up in the Malibu hills and displays Greek, Roman and Etruscan antiques. The villa was designed for wealthy industrialist J. Paul Getty and was intended to recreate the Villa dei Papiri at Herculaneum. Architects Rodolfo Machado and Jorge Silvetti renovated the villa in the 1990s with an eye to preserving its classical style.

Outside of its cities, California impresses even more: The Northern California coastline is populated by imposing redwood trees, also known as sequoia trees. These towering giants can grow more than 365 feet (110 meters) high, taller than the Statue of Liberty, and they live long lives, with many examples between 600 and 800 years old, and the oldest known redwood having reached the ripe old age of 1,200 years. Muir Woods, today a national monument, is filled with redwoods. In 1945, the Charter of the United Nations was drafted and signed there, in a spot now marked by a plaque.

Yosemite National Park in the Sierra Nevada offers more dramatic scenery, including its many waterfalls. At

ABOVE: SILENT FILM STAR NORMA TALMADGE AND ACTOR PETER O'TOOLE (MOST FAMOUS FOR PLAYING THE TITLE ROLE IN LAWRENCE OF ARABIA) ARE JUST TWO OF THE HUNDREDS OF CELEBRITIES WHO HAVE LEFT THEIR HANDPRINTS AND FOOTPRINTS IN THE CEMENT OUTSIDE OF GRAUMAN'S CHINESE THEATER. OPPOSITE: THE HOLLYWOOD WALK OF FAME RUNS DOWN HOLLYWOOD BOULEVARD IN LOS ANGELES.

2,425 feet (740 meters), Yosemite Falls is the tallest waterfall in North America. The park also has glaciers, cliffs, redwood groves and two rivers. Big Sur, located just about halfway between San Francisco and Los Angeles, boasts one of the world's most gorgeous coastlines—rocky cliffs with a sheer drop into the ocean at the spot where the Santa Lucia Mountains soar upward.

The area has campgrounds, a marine sanctuary and several state parks. Gray whales, elephant seals and otters are often sighted off the coast.

The aptly named Death Valley in southeastern California, close to the border with Nevada, serves up another extreme climate—this one dry and hot. The Death Valley salt pan is more than 200 square miles (more than

OPPOSITE: THE GETTY VILLA WAS
MODELED AFTER THE VILLA DEI PAPIRI
AT HERCULANEUM.
P. 214: PALM TREES DOT THE BEACH IN
SANTA MONICA, CALIFORNIA.
P. 215: THE ROLLING HILLS OF THE
NAPA AND SONOMA VALLEYS IN
CALIFORNIA ARE HOME TO NUMEROUS
VINEYARDS.

500 square kilometers) in size. It is the driest and lowest area in North America and the hottest place in the world.

The two states to the north of California along the Pacific coastline, Oregon and Washington, are often overshadowed by their neighbor to the south, but their signature cities, Portland and Seattle—the latter set in picturesque Puget Sound in the very northwest corner of the country—are also lovely small cities with a laid-back style (both are known for their "coffee culture"). Portland, Oregon is home to Powell's Books, the world's largest independent bookstore, which stocks both new and used titles. It also hosts the country's largest outdoor craft market on Saturdays. The Seattle skyline is

ABOVE: THIS JUTTING ROCK FORMATION IN YOSEMITE NATIONAL PARK IS KNOWN AS THE THREE BROTHERS.
OPPOSITE: VERNAL FALL IS A 317-FOOT (97-METER) WATERFALL IN YOSEMITE NATIONAL PARK.
PP. 218-219: SIERRA NEVADA MOUNTAINS ARE REFLECTED IN A LAKE.
PP. 220-221: AT ZABRISKIE POINT IN DEATH VALLEY NATIONAL PARK, CALIFORNIA, EROSION HAS CREATED STRIKING FORMATIONS.

dominated by the Space Needle, built in 1962 for the World's Fair. There is an observation deck at the top. Pike Place Market, a nine-acre market selling fresh and prepared food and other items, was established in 1907.

Both states also have beautiful natural habitats: Crater Lake in Oregon is the deepest lake in the United States at 1,943 feet (592 meters). The Columbia River, which originates in Canada, runs through both Washington and Oregon. Volcanic mountains Mount Hood, Mount Rainier and Mount St. Helens (which erupted violently as recently as 1980) are all massive peaks with hiking trails and glaciers. Olympic National Park in Washington is also a diverse ecosystem. The San Juan Islands in Puget Sound are fertile ground for bikers, hikers and wildlife observers—orcas can be spotted frolicking very close by in the warmer months.

ABOVE: A FERRY DOCKS AT THE SEATTLE, WASHINGTON WATERFRONT.

The only two non-contiguous states in the United States, Alaska and Hawaii, were also the last two to join the union, both in 1959. Both have unique climates and natural settings. Hawaii is an island chain in the Pacific Ocean with several volcanoes, including Mauna Kea and Mauna Loa on the island of Hawaii (often referred to as "the big island" to make clear that it is the individual island being referenced and not the entire state). Molokai, another island, was once a leper colony. Today, Kalaupapa National Historical Park sits on the island's northern peninsula. Pearl Harbor on the island of Oahu was attacked by the Japanese military on December 7, 1941 (when Hawaii was a territory of the United States, but not yet a state), drawing the United States into World War II. The USS Arizona sank, and 1,177 crew members died. Today there is a memorial to the ship in the har-

OPPOSITE: CRATER LAKE IN OREGON
IS THE DEEPEST LAKE IN THE UNITED
STATES.

224

OPPOSITE: THE CROWN POINT
PROMONTORY IN OREGON OVERLOOKS
THE COLUMBIA RIVER.
ABOVE: THE DEER PARK AREA OF
OLYMPIC NATIONAL PARK OFFERS
SPECTACULAR VIEWS.
PP. 218-219: THE USS BOWFIN
SUBMARINE IS NOW A MUSEUM. IN THE
FOREGROUND IS THE WATERFRONT
MEMORIAL AT PEARL HARBOR. EACH
OF THE 52 PLAQUES PAYS TRIBUTE TO A
U.S. SUBMARINE DESTROYED IN
WORLD WAR II.

OPPOSITE: HONOLULU, HAWAII'S
WAIKIKI BEACH IS HOME TO
NUMEROUS HOTELS.

bor. Hawaii has its own native culture—the original inhabitants of the islands were Polynesian—which it works hard to preserve.

Alaska—which borders Canada—also still has a significant indigenous population of various tribes. While the large land mass that constitutes the bulk of Alaska may seem remote, the Aleutian Islands arcing off of it into the northern Pacific Ocean are even more isolated. They are also the westernmost point in the United States. Denali National Park on Alaska includes Mount McKinley, the tallest mountain in North America. The park is populated by wildlife of all different kinds, including bears, moose, and caribou. It is a jewel of the national park system and sits on 6 million acres of land, with only one road running through it.

OPPOSITE: DIAMOND HEAD IS A VOLCANIC TUFF CONE ON THE ISLAND OF OAHU, HAWAII. IT WAS FORMED 300,000 YEARS AGO DURING AN ERUPTION.
ABOVE: THE HALEAKALA VOLCANO COMPRISES MORE THAN 75 PERCENT OF THE ISLAND OF MAUI.

OPPOSITE: ABOUT 5 PERCENT OF THE
STATE OF ALASKA IS COVERED BY AN
ESTIMATED 100,000 GLACIERS.

OPPOSITE: GRIZZLY BEARS GO FISHING
IN ALASKA'S KATMAI NATIONAL PARK.
ABOVE: TURNAGAIN ARM IN COOK
INLET IS SURROUNDED BY MOUNTAINS.

239

Copyright © 2013 Sassi Editore Srl
Viale Roma, 122/b
36015 Schio (Vicenza)
Italy

Text Natalie Danford
Images © Shutterstock except page 40 © Melody Kramer

All photographs are from the Shutterstock online archive except page 40 © Melody Kramer

First published in 2014 by Chartwell Books,
an imprint of The Quarto Group,
142 West 36th Street, 4th Floor,
New York, NY 10018, USA
T (212) 779-4972 F (212) 779-6058
www.QuartoKnows.com

Chartwell Books titles are also available at discount for retail, wholesale, promotional, and bulk purchase. For details, contact the Special Sales Manager by email at specialsales@quarto.com or by mail at The Quarto Group, Attn: Special Sales Manager, 401 Second Avenue North, Suite 310, Minneapolis, MN 55401, USA.

10 9 8 7 6 5 4

ISBN: 978-0-7858-3078-8

For the original Italian edition:
Editor: Luca Sassi
Copy Editor: Irena Trevisan
Designer: Matteo Gaule

Printed in China. SASSI190509CV